TARTANS
OF
SCOTLAND

James D. Scarlett

The Lutterworth Press
Cambridge

SCOTTISH TARTANS
Some Facts and Some Fancies

Tartan belongs to the Highlands of Scotland and did not penetrate into the Lowlands, at any rate to any great extent, much before 1707, when the unpopularity of the Act of Union led Lowland ladies to adopt it as a sign of their disapproval. Nowadays, tartan is so widely looked upon as a national emblem that it is pointless, for any reason other than academic, to attempt to confine it behind that imaginary boundary we call the Highland Line.

Over the years tartan has been carried many thousands of miles from its homeland, principally by the groups of emigrants who left Scotland after the '45 and during the Clearances. They took tartan with them to the new colonies with the result that it grew in popularity and outlived the attempt to stamp it out at home.

Today, the keenest interest in the subject comes from Canada and the United States of America. Most of the tartans designed in these countries can only be described as 'trade fancies' but many are genuine and designed with a serious purpose in view. Traditionalists may find it difficult to sympathise with the element of pseudo-heraldry that creeps into these modern tartans which incorporate symbolic colours, e.g. blue for water, purple for the heather-covered mountains, white for the snowy peaks, which were never used by old-time tartan weavers. But tartan is a live business and these are natural developments.

The word 'tartan' is believed to come from the French *tiretaine* and was used initially to mean a type of cloth and not a pattern. Even in the early years of the nineteenth century the word had a dual meaning and it is this which makes it impossible to determine the age of what is now called 'tartan'. There is a very early reference to 'Helande tertane', purchased for the making of trews for King James V in 1538, but no pattern is mentioned and there is no warrant to assume that because the trews were for a Stewart king they were in the Royal Stewart tartan.

From Roman times onwards, there have been references to the garments of the Celts being 'of many colours', 'marled', 'striped', and, in one case, 'striped across'. These have been quoted as evidence that tartan patterns were worn in those early times. While this was probably so, it is merely wishful thinking to assume that 'striped' always meant tartan.

After the failure of the last great Jacobite attempt to regain the Crown of Great Britain, extremely harsh repressive measures were taken against the Highlanders at home. Among these was the passing, in 1746, of an Act of Parliament that forbade the wearing of tartan or any item of Highland dress other than by soldiers of the Highland regiments of the British army. There are signs that this Act was never wholly effective, but it was naturally more so towards the ordinary people who could not afford a spare suit of clothes and had no place in which to hide illicit garments. As a consequence, most of the old tartan patterns were lost forever. Those that have survived have done so either by accident, by some connection, real or imaginary, with Prince Charles and the Rising, or because they are shown in several collections of family portraits. Of these the Grant portraits, often instanced, are probably the best known. In almost all these cases, the mere fact that the tartans have survived has been all that we can expect, and it is very rare for anything to be known of the origin or history of the patterns.

The Dress Act was repealed in 1782 and tartan began a slow climb back to popularity. Surviving records of one of the largest manufacturers of the time, William Wilson & Son of Bannockburn, show only a handful of patterns in 1800 and as many as 150 in 1820. When, in 1822, King George IV became the first reigning monarch to visit Scotland's capital since Charles I, there was much pomp and ceremony and with it a great tartan explosion. The demand by the Chiefs and their retinues for the 'correct ancient clan tartans' was so great that it was only satisfied by the exercise of great enterprise on the part of the manufacturers.

Most Scottish tartans then are comparatively new, the oldest, generally speaking, going back rather less than three hundred years. A brand-new tartan does not become a bad one until an attempt is made to *delude* people into believing that it is ancient. The trade has to take some of the blame for these delusions which it fosters by calling tartans 'Ancient' and similar names and letting the customer think that these names mean just what they imply.

There are three kinds of colour used in tartans: 'Modern' which are dark and strong with blue scarcely distinguishable from black; 'Ancient' which are light almost pastel shades intended to represent the colours of the old natural dyes; and 'Reproduction' (sometimes called 'Muted') which are dull, generally brownish shades based on the colours of a fragment dug up in the peat on Culloden Moor in 1946. Even within these ranges, manufacturers have their own ideas of colour, as will be

HEADGEAR should be of the proper Highland type, such as the Balmoral bonnet shown here; definitely not a tartan cloth cap or deerstalker.

The JACKET for casual wear can be a battledress blouse, but for more formal occasions a proper kilt jacket is a necessity.

The KILT PIN may be a relic of the days before side straps, when it was used to pin at the waist to hold the kilt up, but it is now only an ornament; it is both unnecessary and harmful to the kilt to pin the apron down.

Originally the only weapon allowed to the Highlander, the SGIAN DUBH is now the only knife he has room for; the rule-makers say that it must be worn in the top of the *right* stocking and have obviously never heard of left-handed people. The top of the stocking is a handy place for carrying pencils, fountain pens and tobacco pipes as well.

The NECKTIE is chosen in the same way as for any other dress; a tweed tie to tone with the jacket is a safe choice.

A kilt has no pockets, and the SPORRAN take their place. A plain hide or fur one is suitable fc general day wear; silver mountings belong to th evening and floor-sweeping horsehair to pip bands. One has to be fairly highly organised to liv successfully in a sporran, and some interna pockets and a small deerskin coin bag help.

The KILT should finish well above the knee, so as to avoid 'sawing' the backs of the knees when wet.

KILT HOSE have a narrow turn down and finish well below the knee; any attempt to sell a kilt and hose that come anywhere near overlapping should be firmly dealt with by the customer. Plain hose are general for day wear, diced and tartan patterns being reserved for the evening. Elastic garters with dummy tabs can be bought, but a more satisfactory substitute is a length of $1\frac{1}{2}$-inch-wide linen webbing taken twice round the leg and tucked under itself.

Highland BROGUES were made of raw deer hide and were probably brown suède, but they were not daintily cut and did not have inch-thick crêpe rubber soles. Generally speaking, stout shoes seem to look best with the kilt; the rules often say that they must be black, but this is a relic of military usage, and there is no reason why taste should not govern choice.

4

seen from the illustrations in this book; it is the pattern of tartan that matters, not the shades of colours.

HIGHLAND DRESS

The kilt is one of the few European national costumes, perhaps the only one, to survive into modern times for everyday wear. At the present time it is coming into increasing use, having successfully outlived Victorian attempts to turn it into a fancy dress.

The earliest form of the present-day kilt was the Belted Plaid, a rectangular piece of material about 6 yards long and $1\frac{1}{2}$ yards wide. This was pleated, belted round the waist and hung roughly to the knee. Its voluminous upper part could be pinned up on the left shoulder to keep it out of the way or used as a cloak if weather conditions demanded.

To the Highlander of old, accustomed to travelling long distances on foot across country, and without shelter even at night, this garb had everything to recommend it, but when 'pacification', as it was called, intruded into Highland life, and people began to work indoors, it became less suitable and little more than an overcoat that could not be removed without completely undressing.

An Englishman, one Rawlinson who operated an ironworks in Lochaber, is generally credited with the invention, in about 1715, of the kilt as it is today. One of the stories about him is that, having adopted the belted plaid for his own use, he felt that it might be improved by removing the top half and called in a military tailor to put the plan into effect. Like most legends, the story has become confused, especially as the tailor is often named as Parkinson, but the objections to its truth are nationalistic rather than logical, and there is no good reason why the first man to feel the need for a kilt should not have been the man to invent it.

The new garment, with a separate plaid, caught on very quickly for it was able to do all that the old one could do and was much less cumbersome into the bargain. Today it remains the best wear for any open-air, rough-country purposes, capable of soaking up great quantities of rain without feeling wet and never dragging at the knees as do wet trousers. It keeps one warm in the winter and cool in the summer, and is readily adaptable to all occasions. It is very difficult indeed to look scruffy in a kilt.

Occasionally, 'rules' are laid down for the proper wearing of the kilt (according to the ideas of the rule-maker, of course), but these have little weight. The only real thing to remember is to wear the kilt as you would any other kind of dress, with propriety and comfort and, above all, never as a fancy dress.

The old dress of the Highland women, the Arisaid, was much on the lines of the belted plaid, but contained far less cloth and was much less pleated. It never developed in the same way as the belted plaid, and the modern equivalent is a pleated skirt with a wrap-over front.

THE CLANS

When translated literally the word 'clan' means 'children' or 'descendants'. It is applied to groups of people claiming descent from a common ancestor and calling themselves his 'children'; the senior member, that is the one most nearly related to the common ancestor, is, in theory at least, the Chief. An important effect of this arrangement was to establish social divisions between clan and clan, rather than between classes. In the eyes of the MacA's, all MacA's were equal and all MacB's inferior to them; as the MacB's could fairly be expected to take the opposite view, a good deal of blood was spilt in the cause of this subject alone.

Food depended upon the land, and the ability of a Chief to hold on to his land depended upon the number of fighting men he could raise, so mutual self-interest often led small, and therefore weak, clans to join larger ones. Sometimes such adherents took the name of the dominant partner, but quite often they kept their own which explains why some people can nowadays wear a tartan that does not bear their own name. Such groups are called 'septs' of the clan. They can also be formed from among the specialist tradesmen of a clan. John MacA the Smith, having been in the game long enough to become, colloquially, John Smith, might then go on to father a sept of Smiths in the Clan MacA.

Large and prosperous clans, such as the MacDonalds who set themselves up as Lords of the Isles, formed branches at clan level, and thus we have MacDonalds of Clanranald, MacDonells of Glengarry and so on.

TARTANS

The *right* to wear any tartan belongs to the bearers of the name or names that go with it, but there has never been an objection to the wearing of a tartan for sentimental reasons. This is evidenced by the celebrated portrait at Dunvegan of Norman, twenty-second Chief of MacLeod, in which the plaid has been identified as Murray of

Tullibardine tartan; Norman's mother was closely related to these Murrays and he spent much of his boyhood with them.

In the early years of the nineteenth century, sheer liking for a pattern played a big part in many people's choice, but nowadays it is perhaps better for those without a tartan to accept one of the universal patterns that are available. Hunting Stewart and Caledonia are both quite acceptable and involve no possibility of giving offence.

The records of the Scottish Tartans Society contain particulars of something over a thousand tartans and, even granting that many of these are almost unheard of and others mere variations of each other, it still follows that in a book of this size many must be left out. Our choice of what to put in has been purely arbitrary,

governed by the need to find clan stories that have not already been done to death and tartan specimens that will give good clear illustrations. To those who are left out, we apologise, and take shelter behind an old Gaelic proverb which has it that 'It is a great thing to have written a book, even a bad one.' The best of books cannot contain everything.

The tartans and tales which follow are arranged in areas, rather than alphabetically as is usual. We hope that the reader will be able to refer to the tartans and their localities quickly and easily, instead of having to hunt through clan maps and long, alphabetical lists of names. We must warn, however, that most of the kilts in the Highlands are still on visitors, so that a kilt, when found, may still not be at home.

The Caledonia tartan

Hunting Stewart

MACKENZIE

The MacKenzies occupy the largest single area of territory in the North and, as one historian is careful to put it, 'ignoring legendary origins', regard themselves as descendants of Colin, progenitor of the Earls of Ross. A later Colin of Kintail was created Earl of Seaforth in 1623, but the title became forfeit when the fifth Earl was attainted after the 1715 Jacobite Rising. The Earldom was restored in 1771, and in 1778 the Earl raised the Seaforth Highlanders from among his clan. The MacKenzie tartan is also the tartan of the Seaforth Highlanders and the Highland Light Infantry.

MACRAE

The Macraes were such ardent allies of the larger MacKenzie Clan that they were known as 'Seaforth's Shirt of Mail'. They had much to do with the Seaforth's rise to power and at various times were Chamberlains of Kintail, Constables of Eilean Donan Castle and Vicars of Kintail. They produced many Gaelic scholars, notably Duncan, who compiled the Fernaig Manuscript of 1688–93. The Hunting Macrae tartan comes from a kilt believed to have been worn at the Battle of Sheriffmuir, 1715.

ROSS

The Gaelic name of Clan Ross is Aindreas, meaning the sons of Andrew. Fearcher, son of the Red Priest of Applecross, was knighted for his services to Alexander II in 1215 and was Earl of Ross by 1226. The earldom passed to the Leslies on the death of the fifth Earl in 1372. The present Chief of the clan is Ross of Balnagowan.

MACKAY

Many of the old Highland Chiefs raised regiments for the service of foreign armies. The MacKays, who at one time were known as the Clan Morgan and the Clan Aoidh, indulged in this to a considerable extent, raising armies for service in Bohemia and later in Denmark. Aeneas, grandson of the first Lord Reay, commanded a MacKay Dutch regiment, settled in Holland and was ennobled as Baron van Ophemert. When the Scottish succession ceased, Baron Eric MacKay van Ophemert became the twelfth Baron Reay.

GUNN

Clan life began about eight hundred years ago and after such a length of time the drawing of the name Gunn from a Norse word meaning war may seem a little fanciful, but there can be no doubt of the warlike character of its bearers. Their outstanding contribution to Highland bloodshed was their feud with the Keiths which began with the abduction of a Gunn heiress upon her wedding day and lasted for some hundreds of years until the Keiths were finally defeated. (Note the similarity to the MacKay.)

MUNRO

First heard of in Easter Ross in the twelfth century, the Munros have chosen to use their military prowess in 'official' wars rather than in inter-clan skirmishes. Apart from providing the first lieutenant-colonel and two of the first captains of the Black Watch, they entered into Continental wars and at one time boasted twenty-seven field officers and at least eleven captains in the Swedish army.

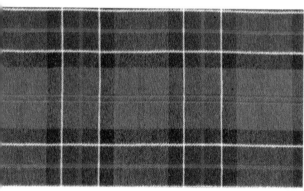

SINCLAIR

The Sinclairs can be traced back to the Norman Conquest. In the twelfth century William de Sancto Claro received the barony of Roslin, Midlothian, and a Sir William Sinclair married Isabella, Countess of Orkney, gaining the earldom of Orkney for his son, Henry; Henry's grandson became Earl of Caithness in 1435. One of the famous men of the name was Sir John Sinclair of Ulbster (1754–1835), an advanced agriculturalist and compiler of the First Statistical Account of Scotland.

CHISHOLM

Chisholm is another Highland clan of Norman origin. The son of Sir Robert De Chisholme founded the line by marrying Margaret, daughter of Weyland of the Aird. James Grant (*The Tartans of the Clans of Scotland*, 1886) tells us that the name occurs very seldom in Scottish history but lists as Chisholms three Bishops of Dunblane, a Comptroller of the Artillery, a Master of the Royal Household and a persecutor of sorcerers, which is not a bad bag even if it is rather mixed.

(Left) Chisholm. The hunting tartan has a brown ground.

CLANS OF THE ISLANDS AND THE WEST COAST

MACDONALD

The islands off the west coast, separated from the mainland by dangerous stretches of water, have come under the influence of true sea-farers and, as a result, many of the island clans are able to claim Norse ancestry. Most powerful among them was the Clan Donald, descended from Somerled, whose Norse name means 'Mariner'. Somerled married Raghnild, daughter of the King of Man, and left three sons, Dugall, Angus and Reginald. Donald, the son of Reginald, gave the clan its name.

Eventually, the clan became so powerful that its Chief was able to proclaim himself 'Lord of the Isles', an action not much to the liking of the King, who felt that there was room for only one King in Scotland and that King ought to be he. In the end, the King won, and John, the seventh Lord, was forced to give up the title in 1494, though not before his son Reginald had founded the mainland branch of Clanranald, from which also derive the MacDonells of Glengarry.

(Right) The MacDonald tartan. Glengarry has a white line centred on the green part and Clanranald takes a white border to the green to match the red border of the blue section.

Legend has it that, at the Battle of Culloden, the MacDonalds were so displeased at not being accorded the privileged position on the right of the line, they refused to charge. Their leader, Alexander of Keppoch, charged alone, calling that his children had deserted him. The truth is that the MacDonalds had to cross 600 yards of open ground, swept by musket fire and grapeshot, before reaching the enemy line and for this reason alone never came nearer than 100 yards from their objective. A fair comment on their behaviour on this day was made by an English sergeant who wrote in a letter to his wife: 'The Rebels, I must own, behaved with the greatest resolution.'

The MacDonalds of Glencoe, or MacIans, have gone down in history as the victims of the Massacre of Glencoe. This occurred in February 1692 when, at the instigation of Edinburgh officials, the soldiers of the Earl of Argyll's Regiment, under Captain Robert Campbell of Glenlyon, fell upon their hosts and murdered nearly forty of the clan. In the Highland mind, the abuse of hospitality is a serious matter, and it is this, rather than the massacre that has left a blot on the name of Campbell for nearly three hundred years.

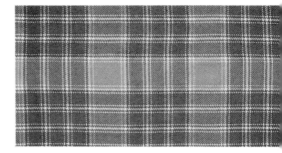

(Top to bottom) MacDonald tartans. Lord of the Isles, a tartan taken from the picture 'The MacDonald Boys', now in the National Portrait Gallery; Lord of the Isles Hunting, from an Armadale painting; MacDonell of Keppoch; MacIan.

MACLEOD

Tormod and Torquil, sons of Leod who was the son of Olave the Black, a thirteenth-century King of Man, were the founders of the Harris and Lewis branches of the Clan MacLeod. Friendship between MacLeod and MacDonald was conspicuous by its absence and their feuds ran fast and furious. The burning of Trumpan Church, complete with its MacLeod congregation who had been locked inside for the occasion, was followed by the Battle of the Spoiled Dykes when the MacLeods wrought equal havoc among the MacDonalds. The dead were so numerous that drystone walls had to be tumbled over the bodies to bury them. In such engagements the MacLeods were lucky to be the possessors of the Fairy Flag which, if waved in time of need, had the effect of trebling the MacLeod numbers, to the discomfiture of the opposition. The flag, which can be seen at Dunvegan Castle, is known to have been used with good effect; some say that it still has one use left.

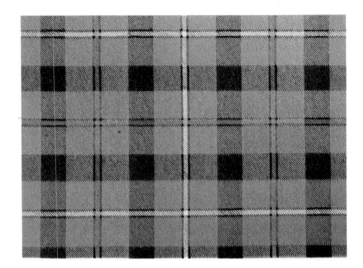

(Top right) The MacLeod tartan, (bottom right) MacLeod of Lewis.

13

MACLEAN

Also to be counted among the major clans of the Islands are the MacLeans, who, in the case of the Lochbuie family, spell the name as it is always pronounced, MacLaine. The Duart and aforementioned Lochbuie branches of the clan remain with us today; both descend from a certain Gillian of the Battleaxe, who flourished in the thirteenth century. The events which followed the '45 Rising impoverished most of the Highland Chiefs and robbed them of their lands but it is pleasant to be able to record that Sir Fitzroy MacLean, the tenth Baronet, was able to repurchase Duart Castle and live in it to the age of 101.

(Top right) MacLaine of Lochbuie. (Right) Hunting MacLean.

MACNEIL

It is often told that a bygone MacNeil of Barra had the charming after-dinner idiosyncrasy of sending his piper to the rampart of Kisimul Castle to proclaim that the great MacNeil had dined and that the rest of the world might now follow suit; an earlier Chief is said to have declined a place in the Ark, as he had his own boat. Historically, the clan settled on Barra by the time of Robert the Bruce. They became tenants under the Lord of the Isles in the reign of David II and received a charter from the Crown when the Lordship became forfeit. General Roderick MacNeil was forced to sell the island in about 1840, but most of it is now back in MacNeil hands and the castle rebuilt.

CLANS OF THE CENTRAL HIGHLANDS

CAMERON

The name Cameron derives from the Gaelic *Cam-sron*, meaning crooked nose. The clan inhabited lands in Lochaber from ancient times and were renowned as fierce fighters which was a useful attribute in days when land was held by the sword. The seat of the Chief, Cameron of Locheil, is at Achnacarry and it was from here that Donald, the 'Gentle Locheil', went to meet Prince Charles in order to dissuade him from his enterprise. Falling under the Prince's charm he joined the Rising instead and suffered with the rest for his loyalty to the Stuart cause.

MURRAY

The Murrays, who take their name from the ancient province of Moray, also were fervent supporters of the Stuarts and it could be said that the '45 Rising would have fared better had the command been left to Lord George Murray who was by far the best, if not the only real soldier among the Jacobite leaders. The Chief, the Duke of Atholl, is of the Tullibardine family, and his seat, Blair Castle in Perthshire, is a noted showplace which is open to the public in the summer months.

STEWART

The origin of the Stewarts, which used to be traced to Banquo, Thane of Lochaber, is now ascribed to one Alan, the Breton Seneschal of Dol. Alan died without issue, but his nephew came to England and later became Sheriff of Perthshire. His third son, Walter, became High Steward of Scotland, whence the name. The 6th High Steward married the daughter of Robert the Bruce, enabling his son to found the Royal line of Stewarts. There are many branches of the clan, widely scattered over central and southern Scotland. The office of High Steward is one of the titles of our present Prince Charles.

(Right) Royal Stewart. (Below, left to right) Old Stewart, an old design, quite different from other Stewart patterns; Stewart of Appin; Stewart of Rothesay, not on sale and not previously illustrated. This comes from a manuscript book in the Royal Library, Windsor Castle, and the author is glad to acknowledge the gracious permission of Her Majesty the Queen to examine and photograph this work; Stewart of Bute.

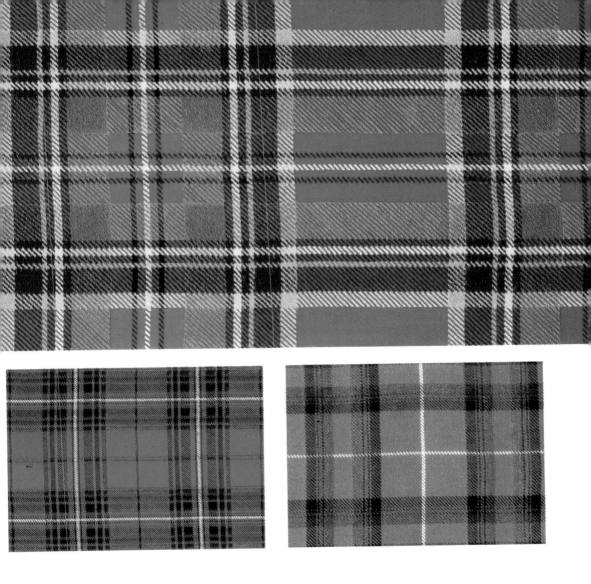

ANDERSON

The name Anderson appears commonly in both the Highlands and the Lowlands, and as it means no more than Son of Andrew, there is little upon which one can pin a line of descent. Some claim alliance with the Rosses, on the grounds that the Gaelic name of the Andersons is *Gille Aindreas* — the servants of Andrew. The tartan is a pretty one, much favoured by the ladies.
(Tartan) Anderson.

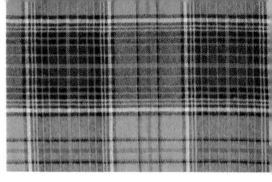

HENDERSON

The Hendersons claim descent from King Nectan of the Picts, although, as an erstwhile Lord Lyon says, 'there is naturally no evidence substantiating this'. They were settled at an early date in the country around Glencoe and it is understood that the direct line ended with an heiress who married Iain, son of Angus Og and progenitor of the Maclans. Up to the death of the last Maclan, the Hendersons had the honour of giving the first lift to the coffin on its way to the burial.

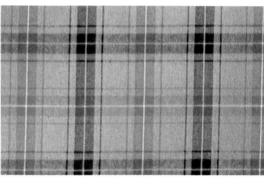

MACGREGOR

In their motto 'Royal is my Race' the Mac-Gregors claim descent from Gregor, brother to Kenneth MacAlpine. A turbulent clan, though perhaps not as black as they were painted, they were heavily persecuted by the law and Campbells alike. At various times they were forbidden even the use of their name and hunted as animals. It was not until 1774 that the suppression of the name MacGregor was finally lifted by an Act of Parliament obtained by John Murray MacGregor.

CUMMING

A companion of William the Conqueror, Robert de Comyn became Earl of Northumberland shortly after the Conquest and his grandson Richard came to Scotland with King David. Among Richard's descendants were the Earls of Buchan and Lords of Badenoch who were first contenders in their own right for the Scottish Crown. They later supported Balliol in the Scottish wars of succession in the fourteenth century but to be on the losing side in those days was always fatal and Bruce's victory rapidly brought about the collapse and extinction of the chief house.

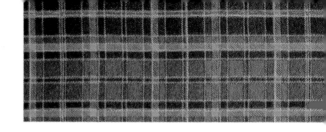

ROBERTSON

The habit of giving by-names was something of an art in early Gaelic society and it is intriguing to imagine what the recipients of these names were really like. How fat for instance was the 'Fat Duncan' from whom the Robertsons take their Gaelic name, *Clan Donnachaidh*? The Robertsons' loyalty to the Stuarts brought eventual ruin and the Chief no longer resides on his ancestral lands. However, the Clan Society has maintained a footing on the ground around Rannoch, and there is a museum at Bruar, near Blair Atholl. (Right) The Robertson and Robertson of Kindeace tartans.

MACMILLAN

Etymologists derive the name Macmillan from Son of the Bald or Tonsured One, and imply an ecclesiastical origin. Prior to the twelfth century the clan inhabited the Loch Arkaig district; later they were settled on Crown land around Loch Tay. In the fourteenth century they moved again to Argyll and Galloway.

(Below, right) The Ancient Macmillan tartan.

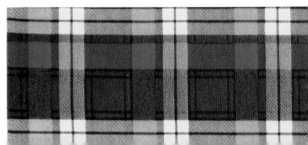

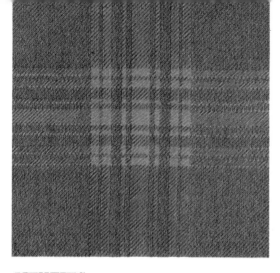

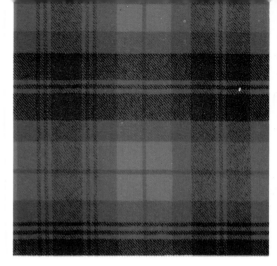

MENZIES

The name Menzies appears in central Perth-shire during the reign of William the Lion although some land was also held in Nithsdale. The name is known in various forms, Menzies, Mengues, Mingies and Meyners. The clan were great planters and Glen Lyon still has many fine trees planted by Menzies of Culdares between 1730 and 1740. The famous Black Wood of Chesthill is largely his work and so too are the rows of beeches and *arboreal mile-stones* – clumps of trees, one tree for each mile – from Meggernie to Fortingall. The first larches in Scotland were also grown on the Culdares estate. Castle Menzies at Weem was put to military use during the 1939–1945 War and later became in danger of complete ruin. It has lately been bought by the Clan Menzies Society who have begun staving off the ravages of time.

MACNAB

One jolly Christmas tale that is told about the Macnabs concerns a Chief who sent his servants for supplies for the festive season. When they returned empty-handed after being waylaid by a band of Neishes, the old Chief uttered the mystic words 'Tonight is the night if the lads are the lads'; his sons, led by Smooth John, went across the hills to the Neish islands in Loch Earn where they all but wiped out the Neishes, taking back the head of old Neish to their father, wrapped in a plaid. An old lady of the district said that she thought the remains of the boat used by the Macnab brothers in their murderous expedition lay on the hill above Loch Tay until as late as 1894. Note: The Black Watch tartan, which is an earlier design, is pat-terned in blue, green and black, in place of the Macnab green, scarlet and crimson.

MACINTYRE

The Macintyres, who stem from the Mac-Donald root, held their lands in Glenoe on Loch Etive from the Campbells of Glenorchy, the tenure being the payment each summer of a snowball and a white calf. All went well until the eighteenth century when a tenant agreed to the payment being commuted to money, after which the rent rose steadily until it could no longer be paid and the clan had to part with its land. The name means 'Son of the Carpenter' and appears fairly regularly among weavers (famous for hose and garters) at Cladich, hereditary foresters to the Lord of Lorne and hereditary pipers to Clanranald and Menzies. Most famous of all the Macintyres was the Gaelic poet, Duncan Ban Macintyre (1724–1812).

MACDOUGALL

The MacDougalls stem from the eldest son of Somerled of the Isles and were settled in the district of Lorne by 1244. Unlike their Mac-Donald cousins they opposed Bruce in the wars of succession and suffered heavily for it although the fifth Chief managed to redeem the family fortunes by marrying a granddaughter of the Bruce in 1344. In their opposition to Bruce, the MacDougalls came close to success for in the pursuit after the Battle of Dalrigh, one of MacDougall's men got close enough to the King to take a grip of his cloak and, although killed for his trouble, managed to tear off the cloak and shoulder brooch. This brooch, which is the famous Brooch of Lorne, is still in the possession of the family.

CLANS OF THE CAIRNGORMS AND THE EAST COAST

CLANCHATTAN

The north-western part of this area belonged almost entirely to the clans making up the great federation of the Clanchattan which was originally composed of the Mackintoshes, Davidsons, Macphersons, MacGillivrays and MacBeans. Like most allies, they were not above fighting among themselves, precedence within the federation and the Chiefship being the usual bones of contention. The latter was finally decided, in law and not on the battle-field, in favour of the Mackintoshes.

MACKINTOSH

This clan's history is one of long-lasting feuds with the Camerons, Gordons, and MacDonells of Keppoch, terminating in the last clan battle of all, at Mulroy, when they were defeated by the MacDonells. A more successful engagement took place one night during the '45, when half a dozen Mackintoshes hid themselves in the darkness and scared off a large Government force by shouting the slogans of different clans. They suffered no loss to themselves and there was only one enemy casualty, Donald Ban, the last of the great piping family of MacCrimmon.

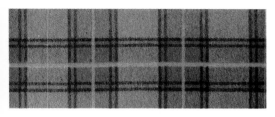

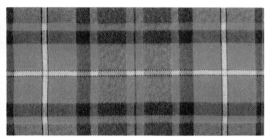

SHAW

The Shaws, formerly of Rothiemurchus, began with a great-grandson of the sixth Mackintosh. James Shaw of Rothiemurchus was killed at the Battle of Harlaw in 1411 and, during the infancy of his son Alasdair, his lands were possessed by the Comyns who built Loch an Eilean Castle. In later life, Alasdair drove out the Comyns and regained his land, but it eventually passed into the hands of the Grants. An important branch of the clan held Tordarroch from 1468 until the nineteenth century.

The tartan (above top), that has been sold under the name Shaw, was taken from a representation of Farquhar Shaw, the Black Watch mutineer, and may be regarded as a faulty reconstruction of the regimental tartan. The new Chief has had designed a tartan (above) more in keeping with the clan's Mackintosh ancestry.

MACPHERSON

Marriage of the clergy was customary in the old Celtic Church, so no slur attached to those called the sons of priests, abbots, monks and parsons. The parson from whom all Macphersons ultimately stem was Muriach, the Celtic Prior of Kingussie and a younger son of a Clanchattan Chief. Muriach's second son set the family on the road to fortune by marrying a daughter of the Thane of Cawdor. Cluny Castle was sold long ago, but many of its treasures were saved by the Clan Association and can be seen in the Clan Museum situated at the junctions of the Loch Laggan and Inverness roads at the south end of Newtonmore.

(Above) Macpherson, the pattern certified as the Clan Tartan by the Chief, 'Duncan of the Kiln', in 1817.

23

DAVIDSON

The Davidsons were known as Clan Dhai after their first Chief, David Dubh of Invernahaven. In the fourteenth century Donald of Invernahaven became associated with the Clanchattan when he married a daughter of Angus, sixth Mackintosh Chief. There was enmity between the Davidsons and the Macphersons from the beginning, apparently over precedence within the Clanchattan. Some historians name the two clans as those who fought the famous battle on the North Inch of Perth in 1396.

MACGILLIVRAY

The MacGillivrays were among the earliest members of Clanchattan and came originally from the west. About 1263 they placed themselves under the protection of the fifth Chief of the Mackintoshes. History has little to say about the clan beyond recording that it took a prominent part in local affairs and became influential. Alexander, the Chief, led the Clanchattan Regiment at Culloden.

MACBEAN

As supporters of the Mackintoshes against the Comyns, the MacBeans fought in many battles and entered into several Clanchattan agreements. Their achievements in battle are exemplified by Gillies MacBean who at Culloden killed fourteen Hanoverian soldiers before he himself fell. In 1858, William MacBean of the 93rd came near to emulating this feat when he gained a V.C. for killing eleven of the enemy single-handed at Lucknow. Major Forbes MacBean of the Gordon Highlanders gained a D.S.O. for his attack on the Heights of Dargai in 1897.

FRASER

The Frasers are yet another clan of Norman stock and are believed to take their name from the Seigneurie of Freseliere in Anjou. Like other Highland clans they were loyal to the Stuarts and were out in the '15 and again in the '45. During the latter campaign, Simon, Lord Lovat gained for himself the name of the Old Fox for his intrigues with both sides. In this he was probably in no way unusual, but he was careless enough to get himself caught, with the usual result.

ROSE

In the Highlands of old the Roses were one of the few clans who managed to remain at peace with their neighbours. Even today their Chief still inhabits the ancestral home. They stem from Geddes in the county of Inverness, and achieved great influence and many important posts through careful marriages. The contents of the family's charter chest are said to be of almost unrivalled interest, both to the private individual and to the antiquarian.

BRODIE

The burning of Brodie House by Lord Lewis Gordon in 1645 has hindered research into the origins of the Brodie family, but it is known that there was a Malcolm, Thane of Brodie in the time of Alexander III and from him descended Alexander, a Senator of the College of Justice. In general, though, the advancement of the family seems to have been by marriage rather than by war; another Alexander, born 1697, became Lord Lyon, and the family has provided three lord lieutenants for the county of Nairn.

FORBES

A Highland stronghold that has all the appearance of a 'fairy castle' is Craigievar, the seat of the Chief of the Clan Forbes (the 'e' is pronounced). The clan's traditional descent is from the great hunter Oconachar who gained fame by slaying a monstrous bear. The first charter however was not received until 1271. There are many branches of the clan apart from Craigievar, including those of Pitsligo, Culloden, Monymusk, Edinglassie and Tolquhoun. Duncan Forbes, the Laird of Culloden, was Lord President of the Council at the time of the '45. He urged common sense upon the Government as a means of quelling Jacobitism but was snubbed for his pains.

GORDON

'Cock of the North' is the march of the Gordon Highlanders and is the by-name of the Duke of Gordon who raised two regiments from among his clansmen. The name is a territorial one from the Border country although it was in Aberdeenshire that Sir Adam Gordon received lands for his service to King Robert the Bruce. Sir Alexander Seton became Earl of Gordon by marriage in 1499 and settled the earldom on his second son who took the name Gordon and was declared Chief of the clan. The fourth Duke and Duchess of Gordon raised the Gordon Highlanders in 1794. Note: Gordon is the regimental tartan and is the Black Watch tartan with yellow lines on the green. A similar tartan with three yellow lines is sometimes called Ancient Gordon.

GRANT

The Grants first appear in the thirteenth century as Sheriffs of Inverness and, like other Highland clans, claim descent from Kenneth MacAlpine. They exerted considerable influence in the north-east of Scotland, were supporters of Wallace and consistently Royalist in their sympathies. In the Jacobite Risings they took the Hanoverian side, except for the Glenmoriston family who remained loyal to the Stuarts. The fine collection of family portraits, including the famous eighteenth-century Piper and Champion paintings, are a splendid source of information about the current forms of Highland dress. They provide an unending supply of ammunition for those who wish to argue about whether there were, or were not, clan tartans before the '45.

MACDUFF

Legend has it that when an old Highland Chief was writing the history of his clan he stopped when he reached the eleventh Chief and wrote in the margin 'about this time Adam was born'. The MacDuffs make no such claims but they are descended from the Celtic Earls of Fife which is a long enough lineage for most people. Although events did not occur quite as the Bard describes them, Shakespeare's MacDuff *was* an historic personage. Among the rewards said to have been given him for slaying Macbeth was the right of his family to set the King on the throne for his coronation. A later MacDuff, Alexander W. G. Duff, created Duke of Fife in 1889, was a founder of the Chartered Company of South Africa.

27

MACNAUGHTON

The MacNaughtons were Thanes of Lochtay in the twelfth century, having apparently been transferred to the district of Strathtay by Malcolm IV. The name is still a common one in the district although the clan later spread to Loch Awe and Loch Fyne. The lands passed out of the family in 1691, upon their forfeiture to the Crown.

BUCHANAN

According to the historian of the Buchanans, the clan is supposed to stem from Anselan O'Kyan, the son of a King of Ulster, who was granted lands in Argyll for his services against the Danes. These lands remained in the possession of the family until 1682, though the Chiefship passed first to the Leny branch and then to the Buchanans of Spittal. The clan supported the Bruce and also the King of France after Agincourt. George Buchanan, the Latin scholar, was tutor to Mary Queen of Scots and James VI, Moderator of the General Assembly and Keeper of the Privy Seal.

(Right, centre) The Buchanan as recorded by James Logan (1831). This is the symmetrical pattern taken from the painting by R. R. Mclan. (Below) The Buchanan as usually made today.

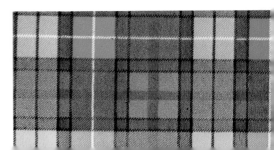

COLQUHOUN

The Colquhouns who take their name from the lands of Colquhoun in the county of Dunbarton, were the first clan to cause trouble for the MacGregors. Following a conference between the two clans, the Colquhouns laid an ambush in Glenfruin, but their intentions were anticipated by the MacGregor Chief, Alastair MacGregor of Glenstrae, and after a bloody battle they were severely beaten and their Chief killed. The outcome of all this was that sixty Colquhoun widows appeared before the King at Stirling, each carrying a bloodstained shirt on a pole. The King gave orders for the extermination of the MacGregors and also for the taking away of their lands and the proscription of their name. They were hunted like animals with no chance of defending themselves, the only weapon allowed them being a pointless knife.

MACFARLANE

Well known for their violent activities in their hunting grounds to the south of Loch Lomond, 'Wild MacFarlane's Plaided Clan', as they were sometimes called, engaged in more ambitious wars as well and claim to have captured three of the Queen's standards when they fought against her at the Battle of Langside. Their generally difficult behaviour earned them the same sort of penalties that were suffered by the MacGregors, but it would appear that the persecution was less vigorously applied or, perhaps, that the MacFarlanes had no especially covetous enemies. Note: The MacFarlane tartan is an interesting colour change from Clanchattan, having green for white, white for yellow and purple for light blue.

CAMPBELL

The branches of the Clan Campbell, who once dominated enormous tracts of land in the southern Highlands, enjoyed an unenviable reputation among their neighbours, and participated to a larger extent than usual in the brutality of ancient Scotland when the quick knife in the ribs, or the hasty hanging without bothering overmuch with a trial, were fairly regular ways of going about things.

The chief house is that of Argyll, and the Chief himself bears the patronymic MacCailean Mor, Son of Big Colin, who was killed in 1294 in a battle at the Red Ford in Lorne. The Earldom of Argyll was bestowed upon Lord Colin in 1457. The eighth Earl was made a Marquis in 1641 and beheaded in 1661. When his son was restored it was again as Earl of Argyll. The tenth Earl was created Duke in 1701.

The Campbells of Breadalbane stem from Black Colin of Glenorchy and rank highest after the Argyll Campbells. They are noted mainly for their persecution of the Mac-Gregors and for their magnificent castle at Taymouth, built on the site of an earlier MacGregor stronghold; MacGregor's Leap, in the narrow Pass of Lyon, marks the spot of an escape, unfortunately only temporary, of a MacGregor chief from his Campbell pursuers.

The third main Campbell line is that of Cawdor, descended from the Thanes of Cawdor by way of the marriage of the seventh Thane with Isabel, daughter of Rose of Kilravock, in 1492.

(Right) Campbell of Argyll is the 42nd Regiment's tartan with the addition of white and yellow overchecks. (Far right, top) Campbell of Breadalbane. (Far right, centre) Campbell of Cawdor, a simpler design than the other two, and one that may be older. (Far right, bottom) The 42nd tartan, often claimed to be a Campbell design.

MACARTHUR

An old Highland saying is that 'there is nothing older unless the hills, MacArthur, and the devil.' The clan is claimed to be an older branch of the Campbells and held the Chiefship until the fifteenth century. Following their support of the Bruce, the MacArthurs received lands in Argyll and the Chief became Captain of Dunstaffnage Castle. When, however, the Chief incurred Royal displeasure in 1427, he was executed and the power of the clan declined. In Skye, a MacArthur family were hereditary pipers to the MacDonalds of the Isles.

GRAHAM

The name of Graham appears regularly in Scottish history from the time of Sir Patrick who was Keeper of Stirling Castle and fell at Dunbar in 1296. Of later times were James Graham, the great Scottish General who fought for Charles I, and John Graham of Claverhouse, the 'Bonnie Dundee' of song and victor at the Battle of Killiecrankie where he was killed in 1689. The Marquis of Graham, afterwards the third Duke of Montrose, gained the repeal in 1782 of the Act which prohibited the wearing of Highland dress or tartan.

CLANS OF THE LOWLANDS

WALLACE

Another great patriot whose name lives on in Scottish memory was Sir William Wallace, the great 'Resistance' leader of the thirteenth century. Wallace showed great military skill but was eventually betrayed and captured. He suffered the usual penalty and was executed in London in 1305. Authority draws the name from among the ancient Britons of the province of Strathclyde, and the family was known in and around Ayrshire in the twelfth century. Among the Wallaces descended from the original family of Riccarton were those of Craigie, of Cessnock, of Kelly and of Cairnhill.

SCOTT

Paradoxically, it was a Lowlander, novelist Sir Walter Scott, author of *Waverley*, who brought the Highlands and the Highlanders to the public eye. Through his romantic tales he helped establish the Highland dress as a popular costume and took an active part in the arrangements made for the visit of King George IV to Edinburgh in 1822. Scott, however, was a sceptic on the matter of clan tartans generally and a firm disbeliever in the existence of Lowland tartans.

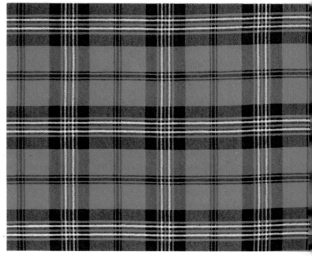

BRUCE

Robert the Bruce, 'patriot king' to the Scots and a thorn in the side of Edward, King of England· who would have preferred a more pliant personality on his northern borders, is famous for having learned perseverance from a spider and for his victory at the Battle of Bannockburn. Like most of the families that achieved early importance, the Bruces are of Norman extraction. The Scottish connection began when Robert de Brus was companion at arms to Prince David during his stay at the English court. When David became King, he granted Brus the Lordship of Annandale. The heart of the famous king, Robert, seventh Lord of Annandale and second Earl of Carrick, lies buried at Melrose Abbey.

DOUGLAS

The origin of the Douglas family who, at one time were among the most powerful in Scotland, is said to be unknown, but the name is usually stated to derive from a Lanarkshire place-name meaning 'black stream'. This name also translates as 'black grey' which may account for the appearance of a Douglas tartan in these shades in 'Vestiarium Scoticum'. The Douglases were originally from the Low-lands and are still largely so, but they spread far and wide and became Earls of Mar, Angus and Douglas. The 'Good Sir James', who carried the heart of Robert the Bruce to the Crusades, was killed in 1330 fighting against the Moors in Spain.

(Above top) The Green Douglas, and (above) Grey Douglas tartans.

ARMSTRONG

n the Border country there were many clans who pillaged and murdered to an extent seldom reached by the men of the North. Chief among these were the Armstrongs of the Liddesdale district. They are said to have been able to muster 3,000 men and their lawlessness kept the border in an almost permanent state of unrest. The situation was largely put to rights when Armstrong of Gilnockie was unwise enough to accept an invitation to meet the King, who forthwith had him and about fifty of his followers arrested and hanged.

NAPIER

A Lowland family of long standing, the Napiers held lands in Dunbarton from 1280. John de Napier helped to defend Stirling Castle in 1303 and William de Napier was Governor of Edinburgh Castle in 1401. William's son, Alexander of Merchiston, was Provost of Edinburgh in 1437; *his* son, Sir Alexander, was Comptroller to James II, Provost of Edinburgh, Vice-Admiral of Scotland and Ambassador to England in 1461. Later, John Napier of Merchiston, born 1550, was the inventor of logarithms and the greatest mathematician of his day.

WHICH IS MY CLAN?

The vagaries of rather primitive spelling, and the 'tapping off' of family names at varying levels of descent, combine to give, in most cases, a very long list of names connected with each Clan. The following list is far from exhaustive and has been further abbreviated by the omission of alternative spellings, except where these are significant. The majority of the Clan tartans referred to are illustrated in colour in this book. Page numbers are given in the Contents list inside the front cover.

Abbot, *Macnab*
Adam, *Gordon*
Adie, *Gordon*
Adamson, *Mackintosh*
Allan, *MacDonald of Clanranald, MacFarlane*
Allardice, *Graham*
Anderson, *Ross*
Andrew, *Ross*

Bain, *MacBean, Macnab, Mackay*
Bannatyne, *Campbell, Stewart*
Bannerman, *Forbes*
Baxter, *Macmillan*
Bayne, *MacKay*
Bell, *Macmillan*
Black, *Lamont, MacGregor, MacLean*
Bontein, *Graham*
Bowie, *MacDonald*
Boyd, *Stewart*
Brebner, *Farquharson*
Buchan, *Cumming*
Burns, *Campbell*
Burnett, *Campbell*

Caddell, *Campbell of Cawdor*
Calder, *Campbell of Cawdor*
Callum, *MacLeod of Raasay*

Carmichael, *Stewart, MacDougall*
Cattanach, *Macpherson*
Caw, *MacFarlane*
Chalmers, *Cameron*
Clarke, *Cameron, Clanchattan*
Clouston, *Sinclair*
Clyne, *Sinclair*
Collier, *Robertson*
Colman, *Buchanan*
Colson, *MacDonald*
Combie, *Mackintosh*
Comrie, *MacGregor*
Comyn, *Cumming*
Conacher, *MacDougall*
Connall, *MacDonald*
Coulson, *MacDonald*
Coutts, *Farquharson*
Cowan, *Colquhoun, MacDougall*
Crerar, *Mackintosh*
Cruickshank, *Stewart*
Currie, *MacDonald of Clanranald, Macpherson*

Davis, *Davidson*
Dawson, *Davidson*
Denoon, *Campbell*
Dewar, *Menzies, Macnab*
Dingwall, *Munro, Ross*
Dochart, *MacGregor*

Donachie, *Robertson*
Donald, *MacDonald*
Donleavy, *Buchanan*
Dowall, *MacDougall*
Dove, *Buchanan*
Duff, *MacDuff*
Duncan, *Robertson*

Edie, *Gordon*
Elder, *Mackintosh*
Ewan, *MacLachlan*

Farquhar, *Farquharson*
Fersen, *Macpherson*
Fife, *MacDuff*
Findlay, *Farquharson*
Finlayson, *Farquharson*
Fleming, *Murray*
Fletcher, *MacGregor*
Fordyce, *Forbes*
Foulis, *Munro*
Frizell, *Fraser*
Fullerton, *Stewart of Bute*
Fyfe, *MacDuff*

Galbraith, *MacDonald, MacFarlane*
Gallie, *Gunn*
Garrow, *Stewart*
Garvie, *MacLean*
Gaunson, *Gunn*
Georgeson, *Gunn*
Gibson, *Buchanan*

Gilbert, *Buchanan*
Gilbertson, *Buchanan*
Gilbride, *MacDonald*
Gilfillan, *Macnab*
Gillanders, *Ross*
Gillespie, *Macpherson*
Gillies, *Macpherson*
Glen, *Mackintosh*
Glennie, *Mackintosh*
Gorrie, *MacDonald*
Gow, *Macpherson*
Gowan, *Clan Donald*
Gowrie, *Clan Donald*
Gray, *Stewart of Atholl, Sutherland*
Gregor, *MacGregor*
Gregory, *MacGregor*
Greig, *MacGregor*
Grier, *MacGregor*
Grierson, *MacGregor*
Grigor, *MacGregor*

Hardy, *Farquharson, Mackintosh*
Harper, *Buchanan*
Harperson, *Buchanan*
Harris, *Campbell*
Hastings, *Campbell of Loudon*
Hawes, *Campbell*
Hawthorn, *MacDonald*
Henderson, *MacDonald of Glencoe*

Hendry, *MacNaughton, Henderson*
Hewison, *MacDonald*
Houston, *MacDonald*
Howison, *MacDonald*
Hughson, *MacDonald*
Huntly, *Gordon*
Hutchinson, *MacDonald*

Inches, *Robertson*

Jameson, *Gunn, Stewart of Bute*
Johnson, *Gunn, MacDonald of Ardnamurchan and of Glencoe*

Kay, *Davidson*
Keith, *Macpherson, Sutherland*
Kelly, *MacDonald*
Kennedy, *Cameron*
Kenneth, *MacKenzie*
Kilpatrick, *Colquhoun*
Kirkpatrick, *Colquhoun*
Kinnell, *MacDonald*
Kinnieson, *MacFarlane*

Lean, *MacLean*
Lennox, *MacFarlane, Stewart*
Linklater, *Sinclair*
Livingston, *Stewart of Appin*

MacAdam, *MacGregor*
MacAdie, *Ferguson*
MacAindra, *MacFarlane*
MacAndrew, *Mackintosh*
Macaree, *MacGregor*
MacAskill, *MacLeod of Lewis*
MacAslan, *Buchanan*

MacAuslan, *Buchanan*
MacAulay, *MacLeod of Lewis*
MacBaxter, *Macmillan*
MacBeath, *MacBean, MacDonald, MacLean*
MacBride, *MacDonald*
MacBurie, *MacDonald of Clanranald*
MacCall, *MacDonald*
MacCash, *MacDonald*
MacCaskill, *MacLeod of Lewis*
MacCaul, *MacDonald*
MacCause, *MacFarlane*
MacCaw, *MacFarlane, Stewart of Bute*
MacCay, *MacKay*
MacChoiter, *MacGregor*
MacChruiter, *Buchanan*
MacCloy, *Stewart of Bute*
MacClure, *MacLeod*
MacCodrum, *MacDonald*
MacColl, *MacDonald*
MacColman, *Buchanan*
MacComas, *Gunn*
MacCombe, *Mackintosh*
MacCombie, *Mackintosh*
MacCombich, *Stewart of Appin*
MacComie, *Mackintosh*
MacConacher, *MacDougall*
MacConachie, *MacGregor, Robertson*
MacCondy, *MacFarlane*
MacConnach, *MacKenzie*
MacConnell, *MacDonald*
MacCooish, *MacDonald*

MacCook, *MacDonald*
MacCorkindale, *MacLeod of Lewis*
MacCorkill, *Gunn*
MacCormack, *Buchanan*
MacCormick, *Maclaine of Lochbuie*
MacCorquodale, *MacLeod of Lewis*
MacCoull, *MacDougall*
MacCowan, *Colquhoun, MacDougall*
MacCraw, *Macrae*
MacCrain, *MacDonald*
MacCrie, *MacKay, Macrae*
Maccrouther, *MacGregor*
MacCuag, *MacDonald*
MacCuaig, *Farquharson, MacLeod*
MacCuish, *MacDonald*
MacCulloch, *MacDougall, Munro, Ross, MacDonald*
MacCurrach, *Macpherson*
MacDaniell, *MacDonald*
MacDavid, *Davidson*
MacDiarmid, *Campbell of Argyll*
MacDonachie, *Robertson*
Macdonleavy, *Buchanan*
MacDowall, *MacDougall*
Macdrain, *MacDonald*
MacDulothe, *MacDougall*
MacEachern, *MacDonald*

MacElfrish, *MacDonald*
MacElheran, *MacDonald*
MacFadyen, *Maclaine of Lochbuie*
MacFall, *Mackintosh*
MacFarquhar, *Farquharson*
MacFater, *MacLaren*
MacFeat, *MacLaren*
MacFergus, *Ferguson*
MacGaw, *MacFarlane*
MacGeoch, *MacFarlane*
Macghee, *MacKay*
MacGibbon, *Buchanan of Sallochy, Campbell of Argyll, Graham of Monteith*
MacGilbert, *Buchanan*
MacGilchrist, *MacLachlan, Ogilvy*
MacGillonie, *Cameron*
MacGilp, *MacDonell of Keppoch*
MacGilroy, *Grant, MacGillivray*
MacGilvray *MacGillivray*
MacGilvernock *Graham of Monteith*
MacGowan, *MacDonald, Macpherson*
MacGown, *MacDonald*
Macgrewar, *MacGregor*
Macgrime, *Graham of Monteith*
Macgrowther, *MacGregor*
Macgruer, *Fraser*
Macgruther, *MacGregor*
MacGuaran, *Macquarrie*
Machardy, *Farquharson, Mackintosh*

37

MacHendry, *Henderson, MacNaughton*
MacHenry, *Henderson, MacNaughton*
MacHowell, *MacDougall*
MacHugh, *MacDonald*
MacHutchen, *MacDonald*
MacIan, *Gunn, MacDonald*
Macilreach, *MacDonald*
Macilleriach, *MacDonald*
Macilrevie, *MacDonald*
Macilroy, *MacGillivray, Grant*
Macilvain, *MacBean*
Macilvora, *Maclaine of Lochbuie*
Macilvrae, *MacGillivray*
Macilvride, *MacDonald*
Macilwraith, *MacDonald*
Macimmey, *Fraser*
Macinally, *Buchanan*
Macindeor, *Buchanan, Macnab, Menzies*
Macindoe, *Buchanan*
Macinroy, *Robertson*
Macinstalker, *MacFarlane*
MacIock, *MacFarlane*
MacIsaac, *Campbell of Craignish, MacDonald*
MacIver, *Campbell, Robertson, MacKenzie*
MacJames, *MacFarlane*
MacKail, *Cameron*
MacKames, *Gunn*
MacKean, *Gunn, MacDonald of Ardnamurchan, MacDonald of Glencoe*
Mackechnie, *MacDonald of Clanranald*

Mackee, *Mackay*
MacKeith, *Macpherson*
MacKellachie, *MacDonald*
MacKellaig, *MacDonald*
MacKellar, *Campbell*
MacKelloch, *MacDonald*
MacKerchar, *Farquharson*
MacKerlich, *MacKenzie*
MacKerras, *Ferguson*
MacKersey, *Ferguson*
MacKichan, *MacDonald of Clanranald, MacDougall*
Mackie, *MacKay*
MacKiggan, *Clan Donald*
MacKillican, *Mackintosh*
MacKim, *Fraser*
MacKimmie, *Fraser*
Mackindlay, *Farquharson*
Mackinlay, *Buchanan, Farquharson, MacFarlane, Stewart of Appin*
MacKinnell, *MacDonald*
MacKirdy, *Stewart of Bute*
Macknight, *MacNaughton*
Maclae, *Stewart of Appin*
Maclagan, *Robertson*
MacLairish, *MacDonald*
MacLardie, *MacDonald*
MacLardy, *MacDonald*
MacLarty, *MacDonald*
MacLaverty, *MacDonald*
MacLaws, *Campbell of Argyll*
Maclay, *Stewart of Appin*

MacLergain, *MacLean*
MacLeish, *Macpherson*
MacLeverty, *MacDonald*
MacLewis, *MacLeod of Lewis, Stewart of Bute*
MacLiver, *MacGregor*
MacMartin, *Cameron*
MacMaster, *Buchanan, Macinnes*
MacMaurice, *Buchanan*
MacMenzies, *Menzies*
MacMichael, *Stewart*
MacMinn, *Menzies*
MacMonies, *Menzies*
MacMunn, *Stewart of Bute*
MacMorran, *Mackinnon*
MacMurchy, *Buchanan, Clan Donald Mackenzie*
MacMurdoch, *Clan Donald, Macpherson*
MacMurray, *Murray*
MacMutrie, *Stewart of Bute*
MacNair, *MacFarlane, MacNaughton*
MacNamell, *MacDougall*
MacNee, *MacGregor*
MacNeiledge, *MacNeil*
MacNeish, *MacGregor*
MacNelly, *MacNeil*
MacNeur, *MacFarlane*
MacNichol, *Campbell*
MacNider, *MacFarlane*
MacNie, *MacGregor*
MacNish, *MacGregor*
MacNiter, *MacFarlane*
MacNiven, *Cumming, Mackintosh, MacNaughton*
MacNuir, *MacNaughton*

MacOmie, *Mackintosh*
MacOnie, *Cameron*
MacOran, *Campbell of Melfort*
MacOwen, *Campbell of Argyll*
MacPeter, *MacGregor*
MacPetrie, *MacGregor*
MacPhail, *Cameron, Clanchattan, MacKay*
MacPhater, *MacLaren*
MacPhedran, *Campbell of Argyll*
MacPhilip, *MacDonald of Keppoch*
Macquey, *MacKay*
Macquoid, *MacKay*
Macquire, *Macquarrie*
MacQuistan, *MacDonald*
Macra, *Macrae*
Macrach, *Macrae*
Macraild, *MacLeod of Harris*
MacRaith, *Macrae, MacDonald*
MacRankin, *MacLean*
MacRath, *Macrae*
Macritchie, *Mackintosh*
MacRobb, *Gunn, Innes, MacFarlane, Robertson*
MacRobert, *Robertson*
MacRorie, *MacDonald*
MacRory, *MacDonald*
MacRuer, *MacDonald*
MacRurie, *MacDonald*
MacRury, *MacDonald*
MacShannachan, *MacDonald*
MacShimes, *Fraser*
MacSimon, *Fraser*
MacSorley, *Cameron, MacDonald, Lamont*

MacSporran, *MacDonald*
MacSwan, *Macqueen, MacDonald*
MacSymon, *Fraser*
MacTaggart, *Ross*
MacTause, *Campbell*
MacTavish, *Campbell*
MacTear, *Ross, Macintyre*
MacThomas, *Campbell, Mackintosh*
MacTier, *Ross*
MacTire, *Ross*
MacUre, *Campbell of Argyll*
Macvail, *Cameron, Mackay, Clanchattan*
MacVanish, *MacKenzie*
MacVarish, *MacDonald of Clanranald*
MacVeagh, *MacLean, MacDonald*
MacVean, *MacBean*
MacVey, *MacLean, MacDonald*
MacVicar, *MacNaughton, Campbell*
MacVinish, *MacKenzie*
MacVurie, *MacDonald of Clanranald*
MacWalter, *MacFarlane*
MacWhannell, *MacDonald*
MacWhirter, *Buchanan*
MacWilliam, *Gunn, MacFarlane*
Malloch, *MacGregor*
Manson, *Gunn*
Martin, *Cameron, MacDonald*
May, *MacDonald*
Means, *Menzies*

Mennie, *Menzies*
Menteith, *Graham, Stewart (Royal)*
Meyners, *Menzies*
Michie, *Forbes*
Miller, *MacFarlane*
Milne, *Gordon, Ogilvy*
Minn, *Menzies*
Monach, *MacFarlane*
Monteith, *Graham, Stewart*
Monzie, *Menzies*
Moray, *Murray*
Munn, *Stewart of Bute*
Murchie, *Buchanan, Clan Donald, MacKenzie*
Murchison, *Buchanan, Clan Donald, MacKenzie*
Murdoch, *Clan Donald, Macpherson*
Murdoson, *Clan Donald, Macpherson*

Napier, *MacFarlane*
Neilson, *MacKay*
Nelson, *Gunn*
Neish, *MacGregor*
Niven, *Cumming, Mackintosh, MacNaughton*
Noble, *Mackintosh*
Norman, *MacDonald*

Paul, *Cameron, Mackintosh, MacKay*
Parlane, *MacFarlane*
Paterson, *MacLaren*
Peter, *MacGregor*
Philipson, *MacDonell of Keppoch*

Pitullich, *MacDonald*
Polson, *MacKay*
Purcell, *MacDonald*

Rae, *Macrae*
Rankin, *MacLean*
Rattray, *Murray*
Reid, *Robertson*
Revie, *MacDonald, Clan Donald*
Riach, *Farquharson, MacDonald*
Risk, *Buchanan*
Ritchie, *Mackintosh*
Robb, *MacFarlane, Robertson*
Robson, *Gunn*
Rorison, *MacDonald*
Roy, *Robertson*
Ruskin, *Buchanan*

Sanderson, *MacDonell of Glengarry*
Sandison, *Gunn*
Shannon, *MacDonald*
Sim, *Fraser*
Sime, *Fraser*
Simpson, *Fraser*
Simson, *Fraser*
Small, *Murray*
Smith, *Clanchattan*
Sorley, *Cameron, MacDonald, Lamont*
Spalding, *Murray*
Spence, *MacDuff*
Spens, *MacDuff*
Spittal, *Buchanan*
Sporran, *MacDonald*
Stalker, *MacFarlane*
Stark, *Robertson*
Swanson, *Gunn*

Syme, *Fraser*
Symon, *Fraser*

Taggart, *Ross*
Tarril, *Mackintosh*
Tawse, *Farquharson*
Tawesson, *Campbell*
Taylor, *Cameron*
Thomas, *Campbell*
Thomason, *Campbell, MacFarlane*
Thompson, *Campbell*
Tolmie, *MacLeod*
Tonnochy, *Robertson*
Tosh, *Mackintosh*
Toshach, *Mackintosh*
Train, *MacDonald*
Tweedie, *Fraser*
Tyre, *Macintyre*

Ure, *Campbell*

Vass, *Munro, Ross,*

Wass, *Munro, Ross*
Watson, *Buchanan*
Watt, *Buchanan*
Weaver, *MacFarlane*
Weir, *MacNaughton, MacFarlane, Buchanan*
Wemyss, *MacDuff*
Whannell, *MacDonald*
Wharrie, *Macquarrie*
White, *MacGregor, Lamont*
Williamson, *Gunn, MacKay*
Wilson, *Gunn*
Wright, *Macintyre*

Yuill, *Buchanan*
Yule, *Buchanan*

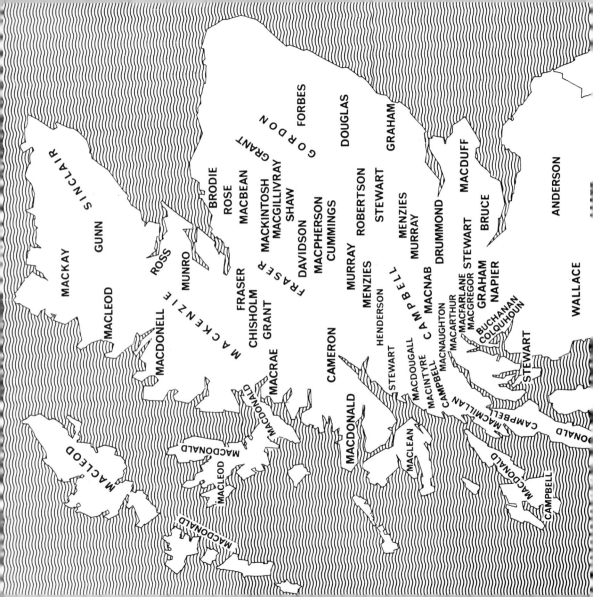